Preface

Welcome to the comprehensive collection of solved papers for the Post Graduate Diploma in Computer Applications (PGDCA) program offered by the Indira Gandhi National Open University (IGNOU). This book is meticulously crafted to assist students in their preparation for the Object Oriented Programming using Java examination, a fundamental and integral part of the PGDCA curriculum. As technology continues to evolve, Java remains a cornerstone of computer science, playing a pivotal role in software development across diverse platforms. Recognizing the significance of a strong foundation in Java programming, this compilation brings together years of previous exam papers with detailed solutions, providing a valuable resource for students to enhance their understanding and excel in their academic pursuits.

Each solved paper within this book is designed to serve as more than just an answer key. Beyond the correct responses, you will find thorough explanations, strategic insights, and helpful tips aimed at aiding your comprehension of Java concepts. Whether you are a novice programmer or a seasoned learner, this collection offers a structured approach to mastering Object Oriented Programming using Java, covering topics ranging from basic syntax to advanced features. The inclusion of previous years' papers ensures that you are well-acquainted with the examination patterns and can approach your assessments with confidence.

As you embark on your journey through the PGDCA program, we hope this book proves to be a valuable companion, aiding you in your quest for proficiency in Java. It is our sincere desire that this resource contributes significantly to your academic success, fostering a deeper appreciation for Java programming and its applications in the dynamic world of computer science. Best of luck in your studies and may this book serve as a stepping stone towards a rewarding and fulfilling career in the realm of computer applications.

Table of Contents

Preface 1

Chapter 1: Term-End Examination, December, 2021 3

Chapter 2: Term-End Examination, June, 2022 5

Chapter 3: Term-End Examination, December, 2022 7

Chapter 4: Mostly Asked Important Questions – Part A 9

Chapter 5: Mostly Asked Important Questions – Part B 11

Chapter 6: Mostly Asked Important Questions – Part C 13

Chapter 7: Mostly Asked Important Questions – Part D 15

Chapter 9: Mostly Asked Important Questions – Part E 16

Chapter 10: Mostly Asked Important Questions – Part F 17

Chapter 11: Mostly Asked Important Questions – Part G 19

Chapter 12: Mostly Asked Important Questions – Part H 21

Chapter 13: Mostly Asked Important Questions – Part I 24

Chapter 14: Mostly Asked Important Questions – Part J 26

Chapter 15: Mostly Asked Important Questions – Part K 28

Chapter 16: Mostly Asked Important Questions – Part L 30

Chapter 17: Mostly Asked Important Questions – Part M 32

Chapter 18: Mostly Asked Important Questions – Part N 34

Chapter 19: Mostly Asked Important Questions – Part O 36

Chapter 20: Mostly Asked Important Questions – Part P 38

Post Graduate Diploma in Computer Application (PGDCA)

Chapter 1: Term-End Examination, December, 2021

MCS-206: Object Oriented Programming Using Java

1. (a) What is Object Oriented Programming? What is an object? How is it created in Java? Explain with the help of an example.

(b) Explain use of "super" keyword in Java programming with the help of an example.

c) Write a Java program to demonstrate how a thread is created in Java. Also set the priority of created thread to 8.

2. (a) What is an Abstract Class? Explain advantages of abstract class with the help of a program.

(b) Explain the use of the following classes in Java programming with the help of example :

(i) Date

(ii) List

3. (a) What is Exception? Why proper exception handling is necessary in Java Programming? Write a program to demonstrate use of multiple "catch" clauses in exception handling.

(b) What is "File" class in Java? List any two methods of "file" class. Also explain use of these methods with the help of a program.

4. (a) What is Polymorphism? What are the different types of polymorphism? Explain how polymorphism helps in code reuse in Java programming with the help of a program.

(b) Write a Java program which takes three numbers as input and displays the largest among these.

(c) Explain why main method in Java is always static

Ans- In Java, the main method is the entry point of a Java program. It serves as the starting point for the execution of the

(d) Differentiate between String and String- Buffer classes in Java.

(e) What is Package in Java? Explain, with example, how a user defined package is created in Java

(f) What is JDBC? Explain use of Driver- Manager class in the context of JDBC.

(g) What is Multithreading? Explain Java thread model with the help of a diagram.

5. (a) What is JavaFX? Explain the features of JavaFX.

(b) What is JDBC batch processing? Explain with the help of a program.

Post Graduate Diploma in Computer Applications (PGDCA)

Chapter 2: Term-End Examination, June, 2022

MCS-206: Object Oriented Programming Using Java

1. (a) What are access specifiers? Explain the difference between public and private access specifiers in Java, with the help of an example.

(b) Write a Java program which takes a string as input and displays its length.

(c) Write a Java program to find the sum of two matrices of dimension 3×3.

(d) What is a package in Java? Explain accessibility rules for packages.

(e) Explain the use of Map class in Java, with the help of a program.

(f) What is object serialization? Explain the working and use of object serialization.

(g) Explain event handling in JavaFX, with the help of a program.

2. (a) What is inheritance? Explain the advantages of inheritance. Explain order of calling of constructors in the case of multilevel inheritance, with the help of a program.

3. (a) What is multithreading? Explain how thread synchronization is achieved in Java, with the help of a
program.

(b) What is polymorphism? Explain the different types of polymorphism that are supported by Java, with the help of examples.

4. (a) Explain how Java provides platform independence, with the help of a diagram.

(b) Explain the use of ''final'' and ''super'' keywords of Java.

(c) What is exception? Explain basic causes of exception. Write a program to explain how to handle "ArrayIndexOutOfBoundsException" in Java. Also explain the use of "finally" clause in exception handling.

5. (a) What is encapsulation? How is it implemented in Java? Explain through a program.

(b) Explain the use of getter methods and setter methods in Java programming, with the help of an example.

(c) Explain the difference between abstract class and interface.

(d) Explain the use of "ByteStream" class in Java.

Post Graduate Diploma in Computer Applications (PGDCA)

Chapter 3: Term-End Examination, December, 2022

MCS-206: Object Oriented Programming Using Java

1.(a) Write a java program which takes three numbers as input and displays average of these numbers.

(b) Briefly explain use of the following logical operators with the help of example of each:

(c) Explain function overloading with the help of a program.

(d) Explain use of abstract class with the help of a program. Explain why abstract class cannot be instantiated.

(e) What is constructor? Explain how parameterised constructors are defined in Java.

(f) Explain use of ResultSet interface in JDBC programming with the help of a program.

(g) Write a Java program to display table of a given number between 1 to 20.

2. (a) What is inheritance? Explain advantages of inheritance. Explain how inheritance in Java is implemented with the help of a program. Also explain the advantages of method overriding.

(b) What is multithreading? Briefly explain how thread is created in Java. Explain use of isAlive() method in multithreaded programming with the help of a program.

3. (a) Write a Java program which takes a string as input and displays reverse of the input string.

(b) Explain different uses of "final" keyword of Java.

(c) Explain advantages of exception handling. Explain how exceptions are handled in Java, with the help of a program. Also explain use of "throws" clause in Java.

4. (a) Explain use of interface in Java with the help of an example program. Also describe difference between abstract class and interface.

(b) Discuss the utility of set and vector classes in Java Programming with the help of a program.

5. (a) What is GUI programming in Java? Briefly explain the features of "AWT" and "Swing" in Java.

(b) Write a Java program using appropriate GUI components, which takes your name and e-mail id as input and displays them on click of a button.

(c) What is JDBC? What is the use of JDBC driver? Explain the steps to connect a database through JDBC.

Chapter 4: Mostly Asked Important Questions – Part A

Q1. What is Object-Oriented Programming, and how is it implemented in Java?

Answer: Object-Oriented Programming (OOP) is a paradigm where programs are structured around objects, which combine data (attributes) and behavior (methods). Java implements OOP principles by using classes to define blueprints and objects as instances of these classes. Java supports encapsulation, inheritance, polymorphism, and abstraction, enabling developers to write modular, reusable, and maintainable code.

Q2. What is the difference between a class and an object in Java?

Answer: A class is a blueprint that defines properties and methods shared by all objects of that type. It exists only in code until instantiated. An object is a runtime instance of a class created using the new keyword. For example, if Car is a class, then Car myCar = new Car(); creates an object myCar based on that class.

Q3. What is encapsulation in Java, and why is it important?

Answer: Encapsulation is the process of hiding the internal state of an object and allowing access only through public methods. In Java, fields are usually marked private, and access is provided via getter and setter methods. Encapsulation protects data integrity, improves code maintainability, and allows controlled interaction with an object's internal state.

Q4. Explain inheritance in Java with an example.

Answer: Inheritance allows a child class to inherit fields and methods from a parent class. This facilitates code reuse and hierarchical organization. In Java, inheritance is implemented using the extends keyword. For example, class Animal { void eat() {} } class Dog extends Animal { void bark() {} } means Dog inherits eat() from Animal and can also have its own method bark().

Q5. What is polymorphism in Java, and how is it achieved?

Answer: Polymorphism allows objects to take many forms and enables a single method or operator to behave differently based on context. Java achieves this through method overloading (compile-time polymorphism) and method overriding (runtime polymorphism). For example, overloading occurs when multiple methods share the same name but differ in parameters, while overriding allows a subclass to redefine a method from its superclass.

Q6. What is abstraction in Java, and how does it differ from encapsulation?

Answer: Abstraction hides complex implementation details and exposes only the necessary functionalities. In Java, abstraction is achieved using abstract classes and interfaces. Encapsulation hides data inside objects and restricts access to it. Abstraction focuses on *what* an object does, while encapsulation focuses on *how* data is stored and accessed.

Q7. What are abstract classes in Java, and when would you use them?

Answer: An abstract class is declared with the abstract keyword and may contain both abstract methods (without bodies) and concrete methods (with implementations). It cannot be instantiated and serves as a base class for subclasses to provide specific implementations. Abstract classes are used when there is shared functionality among classes but also differences that need to be implemented in child classes.

Q8. What are interfaces in Java, and how are they different from abstract classes?

Answer: An interface defines a contract of abstract methods that implementing classes must provide. In Java 8 and later, interfaces can also include default and static methods. Unlike abstract classes, interfaces cannot contain instance fields or constructors, and a class can implement multiple interfaces but can only extend one abstract class.

Q9. What is method overloading in Java, and how does it work?

Answer: Method overloading allows multiple methods in the same class to have the same name but different parameter lists. The compiler selects the appropriate method based on the number, type, and order of parameters. For example, void print(int a) and void print(String s) are two overloaded methods.

Q10. What is method overriding in Java, and what are its rules?

Answer: Method overriding occurs when a subclass provides its own implementation for a method defined in its superclass. The overriding method must have the same name, parameters, and return type (or a compatible one). The access modifier of the overriding method cannot be more restrictive than that of the overridden method.

Chapter 5: Mostly Asked Important Questions – Part B

Q1. What is the difference between static and dynamic binding in Java?

Answer: Static binding happens at compile time when the compiler resolves method calls, as in method overloading. Dynamic binding occurs at runtime when the JVM determines which overridden method to invoke based on the actual object type, enabling runtime polymorphism.

Q2. What is the difference between composition and inheritance in Java?

Answer: Inheritance allows a class to acquire properties and behavior from a parent class, representing an "is-a" relationship. Composition involves creating classes by including instances of other classes as fields, representing a "has-a" relationship. Composition is preferred over inheritance in many cases because it promotes loose coupling and better code modularity.

Q3. What is the difference between final, finally, and finalize in Java?

Answer: final is a keyword used to mark variables as constants, prevent method overriding, or prevent class inheritance. finally is a block that always executes after a try-catch block, whether an exception occurs or not. finalize() is a method invoked by the garbage collector before reclaiming an object's memory, used for cleanup tasks.

Q4. What is a constructor in Java, and how is it different from a method?

Answer: A constructor is a special method that initializes an object when it is created. It has the same name as the class, does not have a return type, and is invoked automatically during object creation. A method, on the other hand, is explicitly called and can have any name and return type.

Q5. What is the difference between shallow copy and deep copy in Java?

Answer: A shallow copy copies an object's fields and references to other objects without duplicating the actual referenced objects. A deep copy creates a completely independent copy of the original object, including duplicates of all referenced objects. Shallow copies are faster but may lead to unintended side effects.

Q6. What is the difference between this and super in Java?

Answer: this refers to the current object, allowing access to its fields and methods. super refers to the parent class of the current object and allows access to parent class members, especially when they are hidden by the subclass.

Q7. What is the difference between abstract methods and default methods in interfaces?

Answer: Abstract methods declare behavior without providing an implementation and must be implemented by any class that implements the interface. Default methods, introduced in Java 8, allow interfaces to provide a standard implementation that classes can use or override.

Q8. What is the difference between method overloading and method overriding?

Answer: Method overloading occurs within the same class when multiple methods have the same name but different parameter lists. Method overriding occurs between a parent and child class when a subclass provides its own implementation for a method already defined in the parent class.

Q9. What is the difference between static methods and instance methods in Java?

Answer: Static methods belong to the class and can be called without creating an instance. Instance methods belong to objects and require an object to be invoked. Static methods cannot access instance variables directly because they do not belong to any specific object.

Q10. What is the difference between an interface and a marker interface in Java?

Answer: An interface contains method declarations that implementing classes must define. A marker interface is an interface without any methods or fields and serves as metadata to signal special behavior to the JVM or libraries. For example, Serializable is a marker interface used to indicate that an object can be serialized.

Chapter 6: Mostly Asked Important Questions – Part C

Q1. What is the difference between a static nested class and an inner class in Java?

Answer: A static nested class does not have access to the instance variables of the outer class and behaves like a top-level class. An inner class is associated with an instance of the outer class and has access to its instance variables and methods.

Q2. What is the difference between compile-time and run-time polymorphism in Java?

Answer: Compile-time polymorphism is achieved through method overloading, where the compiler resolves which method to call based on parameter types. Run-time polymorphism is achieved through method overriding, where the JVM determines which method implementation to invoke based on the object's actual type.

Q3. What are access modifiers in Java?

Answer: Access modifiers specify the visibility of classes, methods, and variables. Examples include public, private, protected, and default (no modifier).

Q4. What is the difference between public, private, and protected in Java?

Answer: public allows access from anywhere, private restricts access within the same class, and protected allows access within the same package and subclasses.

Q5. What is dynamic method dispatch in Java?

Answer: Dynamic method dispatch is the process of selecting which implementation of an overridden method to call at runtime.

Q6. What is a constructor in Java?

Answer: A constructor is a special method that is called when an object is created and is used to initialize the object.

Q7. What is the difference between shallow copy and deep copy in Java?

Answer: A shallow copy copies references to objects, while a deep copy creates independent copies of objects.

Q8. What is the difference between aggregation and composition in Java?

Answer: Aggregation represents a weak association where the child can exist independently of the parent, while composition represents a strong association where the child cannot exist without the parent.

Q9. What is the difference between an abstract class and a concrete class in Java?

Answer: An abstract class cannot be instantiated and may have abstract methods, while a concrete class can be instantiated and provides implementations for all its methods.

Q10. What is multiple inheritance in Java?

Answer: Java does not support multiple inheritance with classes to avoid ambiguity, but it can be achieved using interfaces.

Chapter 7: Mostly Asked Important Questions – Part D

Q1. What is a marker interface in Java?

Answer: A marker interface does not contain any methods or fields. It is used to provide metadata to classes, such as Serializable.

Q2. What is the difference between runtime polymorphism and compile-time polymorphism in Java?

Answer: Runtime polymorphism is achieved through method overriding, while compile-time polymorphism is achieved through method overloading.

Q3. What is a package in Java?

Answer: A package is a namespace that organizes a set of related classes and interfaces.

Q4. What is the difference between this and super keywords in Java?

Answer: this refers to the current instance of a class, while super refers to the immediate parent class.

Q5. What is the difference between overloading and overriding in Java?

Answer: Overloading happens at compile-time with methods of the same name but different parameters, while overriding happens at runtime when a subclass provides its own implementation of a method.

Q6. What is the difference between an instance variable and a class variable in Java?

Answer: An instance variable belongs to an object and has a separate copy for each instance, while a class variable (declared static) is shared across all instances.

Q7. What is the difference between composition and aggregation in Java?

Answer: In composition, the contained object cannot exist without the container class, while in aggregation, the contained object can exist independently.

Q8. What is a static block in Java?

Answer: A static block is used to initialize static variables. It is executed when the class is loaded into memory.

Q9. What is a singleton class in Java?

Answer: A singleton class allows only one instance of itself to be created during the lifetime of an application.

Q10. What is the difference between final, finally, and finalize() in Java?

Answer: final is a keyword for declaring constants, preventing inheritance or overriding. finally is used in exception handling to execute code regardless of exceptions. finalize() is a method called by the garbage collector before destroying an object.

Chapter 9: Mostly Asked Important Questions – Part E

Q1. What is object cloning in Java?

Answer: Object cloning is creating an exact copy of an object using the clone() method from the Object class.

Q2. What is the difference between a Java Bean and a regular class?

Answer: A Java Bean is a reusable software component that follows conventions like having private properties with public getter and setter methods and a no-argument constructor.

Q3. What is the difference between an interface and an abstract class in Java?

Answer: Interfaces are used to achieve full abstraction and support multiple inheritance, while abstract classes can have method implementations and do not support multiple inheritance.

Q4. What is the diamond problem in Java?

Answer: The diamond problem occurs with multiple inheritance when two parent classes have the same method, leading to ambiguity. Java avoids it by not supporting multiple inheritance with classes.

Q5. What is method hiding in Java?

Answer: Method hiding occurs when a static method in a subclass has the same signature as a static method in the parent class.

Q6. What is a transient variable in Java?

Answer: A transient variable is not serialized during the serialization process.

Q7. What is the difference between an immutable class and a mutable class in Java?

Answer: An immutable class (like String) does not allow its state to be changed after creation, while a mutable class allows modification of its state.

Q8. What is the purpose of the instanceof operator in Java?

Answer: The instanceof operator is used to test whether an object is an instance of a specific class or implements a specific interface.

Q9. What is a static import in Java?

Answer: Static import allows you to use static members of a class without qualifying them with the class name.

Q10. What is the difference between abstract and final in Java?

Answer: abstract indicates a method or class that must be implemented or extended, while final prevents a method from being overridden or a class from being subclassed.

Chapter 10: Mostly Asked Important Questions – Part F

Q1. What is the difference between composition and inheritance in Java? When should composition be preferred over inheritance?

Answer: Inheritance represents an "is-a" relationship where a subclass inherits the properties and behaviors of a superclass. Composition represents a "has-a" relationship where a class contains an instance of another class. Composition is preferred when flexibility is needed or when you want to avoid tight coupling.

Q2. How does Java achieve polymorphism, and what is the difference between compile-time and runtime polymorphism?

Answer: Java achieves polymorphism through method overloading (compile-time) and method overriding (runtime). Compile-time polymorphism is resolved during compilation, while runtime polymorphism is resolved during program execution based on the actual object type.

Q3. Explain the concept of encapsulation in Java with an example. Why is it important?

Answer: Encapsulation hides an object's data by making fields private and providing public getter and setter methods. It ensures controlled access and protects data integrity. Example:

java

CopyEdit

```
class Person {
  private String name;

  public String getName() {
    return name;
  }

  public void setName(String name) {
    this.name = name;
  }
}
```

Q4. What is the difference between abstract classes and interfaces in Java?

Answer: Abstract classes can have both abstract and concrete methods and instance variables. Interfaces only allow abstract methods (except default and static methods since Java 8) and cannot have instance variables. Interfaces are ideal for full abstraction and achieving multiple inheritance.

Q5. What is the purpose of the super **keyword in Java? Give an example.**

Answer: The super keyword refers to the parent class and is used to call parent class constructors, methods, or variables.

Example:

java

CopyEdit

```
class Parent {
  void show() {
    System.out.println("Parent class");
  }
}

class Child extends Parent {
  void show() {
    super.show(); // Calls Parent's show()
    System.out.println("Child class");
  }
}
```

Q6. What is a static block in Java? When is it executed?

Answer: A static block is used for initializing static variables. It runs only once when the class is loaded into memory by the JVM, before any object creation.

Q7. What is method hiding in Java? How is it different from method overriding?

Answer: Method hiding occurs when a subclass defines a static method with the same signature as a static method in the parent class. Unlike overriding, method hiding is resolved at compile time and depends on the reference type, not the object type.

Q8. What are wrapper classes in Java, and why are they used?

Answer: Wrapper classes (e.g., Integer, Double) allow primitive types to be used as objects. They are necessary for working with collections like ArrayList and for features like autoboxing and unboxing.

Q9. What is the difference between final, finally, and finalize() in Java?

Answer:

final: Used to declare constants, prevent method overriding, and inheritance.
finally: A block that executes after try-catch, regardless of exceptions.
finalize(): A method called by the garbage collector before destroying an object.

Q10. What is the difference between shallow copy and deep copy in Java?

Answer: A shallow copy duplicates the object but shares references of nested objects, while a deep copy creates a complete independent copy, including all nested objects.

Chapter 11: Mostly Asked Important Questions – Part G

Q1. What is the difference between method overloading and method overriding in Java?
Answer: Method overloading happens when multiple methods in the same class have the same name but different parameter lists. It is resolved at compile-time. Method overriding occurs when a subclass provides a specific implementation of a method already defined in its parent class. It is resolved at runtime.

Q2. What is the purpose of the this keyword in Java? Give an example.
Answer: The this keyword refers to the current object of the class. It is used to differentiate instance variables from local variables or to call other constructors in the same class. Example:

```java
java
CopyEdit
class Example {
  private int value;

  Example(int value) {
    this.value = value; // Refers to instance variable
  }
}
```

Q3. What is the difference between a static variable and an instance variable in Java?
Answer: A static variable belongs to the class and is shared by all instances of that class. An instance variable belongs to a specific object, and each object has its own copy.

Q4. What are default methods in Java interfaces? Why were they introduced?
Answer: Default methods are methods in interfaces with a default implementation. They were introduced in Java 8 to allow interfaces to evolve without breaking classes that already implement them.

Q5. What is the difference between an abstract method and a concrete method in Java?
Answer: An abstract method has no body and must be implemented by subclasses. A concrete method has a defined implementation and can be used directly by classes.

Q6. What is the difference between a static method and a non-static method in Java?
Answer: A static method belongs to the class and can be called without creating an object. A non-static method belongs to an instance of the class and requires an object to be invoked.

Q7. What is a constructor in Java, and how is it different from a method?

Answer: A constructor is a special method used to initialize objects and does not have a return type. It is automatically called when an object is created, unlike regular methods which must be called explicitly.

Q8. What is the purpose of the instanceof operator in Java?

Answer: The instanceof operator checks whether an object is an instance of a specific class or implements a particular interface.

Q9. What is a final variable in Java? How is it different from a static final variable?

Answer: A final variable's value cannot be changed once assigned. A static final variable is constant across all instances and belongs to the class rather than to any specific object.

Q10. What is the difference between checked and unchecked exceptions in Java?

Answer: Checked exceptions are checked at compile-time and must be handled using try-catch or declared with throws. Unchecked exceptions occur at runtime and do not require explicit handling.

Chapter 12: Mostly Asked Important Questions – Part H

Q1. What is the difference between method overloading and method overriding in Java?
Answer: Method overloading happens when multiple methods in the same class have the same name but different parameter lists (number, type, or order of parameters). It is resolved at compile-time and is also called static polymorphism. Method overriding occurs when a subclass provides a specific implementation for a method already defined in its parent class. It is resolved at runtime, allowing dynamic method dispatch. Overriding is used for achieving runtime polymorphism, whereas overloading is used to increase the readability of the program by reusing method names.
Q2. What is the purpose of the this keyword in Java? Give an example.
Answer: The this keyword in Java refers to the current object of the class. It is primarily used to resolve ambiguity between instance variables and local variables when they share the same name. It can also be used to call other constructors in the same class (this()), pass the current object as a parameter, and return the current object from a method.
Example:

java
CopyEdit

```
class Student {
  private String name;

  Student(String name) {
    this.name = name; // Resolves naming conflict
  }

  void display() {
    System.out.println("Name: " + this.name);
  }
}
```

Q3. What is the difference between a static variable and an instance variable in Java?
Answer: A static variable belongs to the class and is shared by all instances of that class. It is initialized only once, at the time of class loading, and retains its value across all objects. An instance variable, on the other hand, belongs to a specific object, and each object gets its own copy of instance variables. Static variables are often used for constants and shared data, whereas instance variables represent the unique state of an object.
Q4. What are default methods in Java interfaces? Why were they introduced?

Answer: Default methods in Java interfaces are methods with a default implementation. They were introduced in Java 8 to enable developers to add new methods to interfaces without breaking the classes that already implement those interfaces. Before Java 8, any change to an interface required updating all implementing classes, but with default methods, backward compatibility is maintained. This also allows interfaces to behave more like abstract classes.

Q5. What is the difference between an abstract method and a concrete method in Java?

Answer: An abstract method is declared without a body and must be implemented by subclasses. It is used when the parent class wants to enforce certain methods in its subclasses. A concrete method has a defined implementation and can be directly used or overridden by subclasses if necessary. Abstract methods are used to achieve abstraction, while concrete methods provide default behavior that may or may not be modified.

Q6. What is the difference between a static method and a non-static method in Java?

Answer: A static method belongs to the class rather than any specific instance and can be called without creating an object. It can only access other static members (variables or methods) directly. A non-static method belongs to an instance of the class and requires an object to be invoked. It can access both static and non-static members. Static methods are often used for utility or helper functions, whereas non-static methods operate on the state of specific objects.

Q7. What is a constructor in Java, and how is it different from a method?

Answer: A constructor in Java is a special method that is called when an object is created. It has the same name as the class and does not have a return type, not even void. Constructors are used to initialize the state of an object. Unlike methods, constructors cannot be called explicitly and are automatically invoked during object creation. A method, on the other hand, is used to perform specific operations and must be called explicitly.

Q8. What is the purpose of the instanceof operator in Java?

Answer: The instanceof operator is used to test whether an object is an instance of a particular class or implements a specific interface. It is helpful in avoiding ClassCastException by verifying the type of an object before casting. For example:

java

CopyEdit

```
if (obj instanceof String) {
   String str = (String) obj; // Safe cast
}
```

Q9. What is a final variable in Java? How is it different from a static final variable?

Answer: A final variable in Java can be assigned only once, and its value cannot be changed after assignment. A static final variable is a constant that belongs to the class and is shared across all instances. It is initialized only once, typically at the time of declaration or inside a static block. Final variables enforce immutability, while static final variables combine immutability with class-level scope.

Q10. What is the difference between checked and unchecked exceptions in Java?

Answer: Checked exceptions are exceptions that are checked at compile-time. The compiler ensures that these exceptions are either handled using try-catch blocks or declared in the method signature with the throws keyword. Examples include IOException and SQLException. Unchecked exceptions are not checked at compile-time and typically represent programming errors like NullPointerException and ArithmeticException. They are subclasses of RuntimeException.

Chapter 13: Mostly Asked Important Questions – Part I

Q1. What is the difference between an abstract class and an interface in Java?

Answer: An abstract class can have both abstract methods (without implementation) and concrete methods (with implementation), as well as instance variables and constructors. Interfaces, on the other hand, are fully abstract by default and can only contain abstract methods (until Java 8 introduced default and static methods). Interfaces cannot have instance variables or constructors. Abstract classes are used when you want to share some code among subclasses, while interfaces are ideal for defining a contract that multiple unrelated classes can implement.

Q2. What is the difference between super() and this() in Java?

Answer: super() is used to call a constructor of the immediate parent class, whereas this() is used to call another constructor in the same class. Both must be the first statement in a constructor if used. super() helps in reusing the parent's constructor logic, and this() helps in constructor chaining within the same class.

Q3. What are access modifiers in Java? Explain with examples.

Answer: Access modifiers define the visibility of classes, methods, and variables. public allows access from anywhere. private restricts access to within the same class. protected allows access within the same package and by subclasses. Default (no modifier) allows access only within the same package.

Example:

java

CopyEdit

```
public class Example {
   private int a; // accessible only within this class
   protected int b; // accessible within package and subclasses
   public int c; // accessible from anywhere
}
```

Q4. What is constructor overloading in Java? Why is it useful?

Answer: Constructor overloading occurs when a class has multiple constructors with different parameter lists. It allows objects to be created in different ways. Constructor overloading improves flexibility and makes it easier to initialize objects with varying levels of detail.

Q5. What is the purpose of the final keyword in Java?

Answer: The final keyword is used to declare constants, prevent method overriding, and prevent class inheritance. A final variable cannot be reassigned, a final method cannot be overridden by subclasses, and a final class cannot be extended. This is useful for ensuring certain parts of your code are not modified unintentionally.

Q6. What is static binding and dynamic binding in Java?

Answer: Static binding happens at compile-time and is used for overloaded methods and static methods. Dynamic binding happens at runtime and is used for overridden methods in the case of polymorphism. Static binding is faster but less flexible, while dynamic binding allows the JVM to decide the appropriate method implementation based on the object's actual type at runtime.

Q7. What is a singleton class in Java? How can it be implemented?

Answer: A singleton class allows only one instance of itself to be created throughout the lifetime of the application. It can be implemented by making the constructor private and providing a static method to return the single instance.

Example:

java

CopyEdit

```
class Singleton {
    private static Singleton instance = new Singleton();

    private Singleton() {}

    public static Singleton getInstance() {
        return instance;
    }
}
```

Q8. What is the purpose of the transient keyword in Java?

Answer: The transient keyword is used to indicate that a variable should not be serialized. When an object is serialized, transient fields are skipped and not saved in the byte stream. This is useful for sensitive data or temporary fields.

Q9. What is the difference between == and .equals() in Java?

Answer: == checks if two references point to the exact same object in memory. .equals() checks whether two objects are logically equivalent (i.e., whether their data is the same). For example, two different String objects with the same text would return true with .equals() but false with == unless they are interned.

Q10. What is the difference between aggregation and composition in Java?

Answer: Both represent relationships between classes, but in aggregation, the child object can exist independently of the parent object (weak relationship). In composition, the child object cannot exist without the parent (strong relationship). For example, a "department" has "teachers" (aggregation), but a "house" has "rooms" (composition).

Chapter 14: Mostly Asked Important Questions – Part J

Q1. What is the difference between shallow copy and deep copy in Java?

Answer: A shallow copy creates a new object but does not create copies of the objects referenced by the original object. Instead, it copies the references, meaning changes to the referenced objects in one copy will reflect in the other. A deep copy creates a new object and also recursively copies all objects referenced by the original, so the two objects are fully independent.

Q2. What is method hiding in Java and how is it different from method overriding?

Answer: Method hiding occurs when a subclass defines a static method with the same signature as a static method in the parent class. Unlike overriding, method hiding is resolved at compile-time and depends on the reference type, not the object type. In method overriding, the method resolution happens at runtime based on the actual object.

Q3. What is the difference between a static block and an instance block in Java?

Answer: A static block is executed only once when the class is loaded into memory and is used to initialize static variables. An instance block runs every time a new object is created and is executed before the constructor. Static blocks are used for class-level initialization, whereas instance blocks are used for object-level initialization.

Q4. What is autoboxing and unboxing in Java?

Answer: Autoboxing is the automatic conversion of a primitive type into its corresponding wrapper class object (e.g., converting int to Integer). Unboxing is the reverse process where the wrapper class object is converted back to its primitive type. These features simplify working with collections and APIs that expect objects instead of primitive types.

Q5. What is the difference between throw and throws in Java?

Answer: The throw keyword is used to explicitly throw an exception in the code. The throws keyword is used in a method declaration to indicate that the method may throw one or more exceptions. throw is used for actual exception handling, while throws is used for declaring potential exceptions.

Q6. What are marker interfaces in Java? Give examples.

Answer: A marker interface is an interface that does not contain any methods or fields. It is used to provide metadata or tagging information to classes so that the JVM or frameworks can identify them for special behavior. Examples include Serializable, Cloneable, and Remote.

Q7. What is a transient variable in Java and when would you use it?

Answer: A transient variable is a variable that is not serialized when the object is converted to a byte stream. It is useful when you want to exclude sensitive information or temporary data from serialization. For example, passwords or session-related fields can be marked as transient.

Q8. What is the diamond problem in Java and how does Java resolve it?

Answer: The diamond problem occurs in multiple inheritance when a class inherits from two classes that have a common superclass, leading to ambiguity about which inherited method to use. Java avoids this problem by not allowing multiple inheritance of classes. Instead, it supports multiple inheritance of interfaces, and if two interfaces have conflicting default methods, the implementing class must resolve the conflict by overriding the method.

Q9. What is dynamic method dispatch in Java?

Answer: Dynamic method dispatch is a mechanism by which a call to an overridden method is resolved at runtime rather than compile-time. This allows Java to support runtime polymorphism. The JVM determines the actual method to invoke based on the object's runtime type, not the reference type.

Q10. What is object cloning in Java? How can you achieve it?

Answer: Object cloning is the process of creating an exact copy of an object. In Java, this is achieved by implementing the Cloneable interface and overriding the clone() method from the Object class. By default, clone() performs a shallow copy, but you can customize it for deep copies.

Chapter 15: Mostly Asked Important Questions – Part K

Q1. What is the difference between static and dynamic polymorphism in Java?

Answer: Static polymorphism, also known as compile-time polymorphism, is achieved through method overloading where the method to be invoked is determined at compile-time. Dynamic polymorphism, or runtime polymorphism, is achieved through method overriding where the method call is resolved at runtime based on the actual object type. Overloading improves readability, while overriding enables flexibility in behavior.

Q2. What is the purpose of the finalize() method in Java?

Answer: The finalize() method is called by the garbage collector before an object is destroyed. It is used to perform cleanup operations such as releasing resources. However, it is not guaranteed to run and is generally avoided in favor of try-with-resources or explicit resource management.

Q3. What is a factory method in Java? How does it differ from a constructor?

Answer: A factory method is a static method that returns an instance of a class. Unlike constructors, factory methods can return instances of any subtype or even cached instances. They provide more flexibility than constructors, allowing control over object creation, lazy initialization, and hiding implementation details.

Q4. What is the difference between an inner class and an anonymous inner class in Java?

Answer: An inner class is a class defined within another class and can be instantiated normally. An anonymous inner class is a special type of inner class without a name, declared and instantiated in a single statement. Anonymous inner classes are often used to implement interfaces or extend classes on the fly, typically in event handling.

Q5. What is the difference between public, private, protected, and default access modifiers in Java?

Answer:- Public allows access from anywhere.

- Private allows access only within the same class.
- Protected allows access within the same package and from subclasses.
- Default (no modifier) allows access only within the same package.

These modifiers control the visibility and encapsulation of class members.

Q6. What is a static nested class in Java and how is it different from a regular inner class?

Answer: A static nested class is a static class defined within another class. It does not have access to the instance variables of the outer class unless an instance of the outer class is passed. A regular inner class, on the other hand, is associated with an instance of the outer class and has access to its instance variables and methods.

Q7. What is a functional interface in Java? Give an example.

Answer: A functional interface is an interface with exactly one abstract method. It can have default and static methods. Functional interfaces are used as targets for lambda expressions and method references.

Example:

java

CopyEdit

```
@FunctionalInterface
interface MyFunction {
   void execute();
}
```

Q8. What is the use of the volatile keyword in Java?

Answer: The volatile keyword ensures that changes to a variable are always visible to all threads. It prevents threads from caching the variable's value locally and forces them to read it directly from the main memory. It is used in multithreaded programming for variables that are accessed by multiple threads.

Q9. What is the difference between HashMap and Hashtable in Java?

Answer: HashMap is not synchronized and allows one null key and multiple null values, making it faster but not thread-safe. Hashtable is synchronized, does not allow any null key or value, and is thread-safe but slower. In modern code, HashMap is preferred with external synchronization if needed.

Q10. What is the difference between Serializable and Externalizable interfaces in Java?

Answer: Serializable is a marker interface that allows the default serialization mechanism. Externalizable extends Serializable and requires the class to implement two methods: writeExternal() and readExternal(), giving complete control over the serialization process.

Chapter 16: Mostly Asked Important Questions – Part L

Q1. What is the difference between checked and unchecked exceptions in Java?

Answer: Checked exceptions are exceptions that are checked at compile-time. The compiler ensures that these exceptions are either handled using try-catch blocks or declared in the method signature with the throws keyword. Examples include IOException and SQLException. Unchecked exceptions are not checked at compile-time and occur during runtime. They include exceptions like NullPointerException and ArithmeticException, which are subclasses of RuntimeException.

Q2. What is the purpose of the super keyword in Java? Give an example.

Answer: The super keyword is used to refer to the immediate parent class object. It can be used to call parent class methods, access parent class variables, and invoke parent class constructors. Example:

java

CopyEdit

```
class Parent {
void display() {
System.out.println("Parent display");
}
}
class Child extends Parent {
void display() {
super.display();
System.out.println("Child display");
}
}
```

Q3. What is the difference between == and .equals() in Java when comparing objects?

Answer: The == operator compares object references to check whether they point to the same memory location. The .equals() method compares the contents of two objects to determine if they are logically equivalent. For example, two different String objects with the same text will return true with .equals() but false with ==.

Q4. What is object immutability in Java? How can you create an immutable class?

Answer: An immutable object is one whose state cannot be changed after it is created. To create an immutable class, declare the class as final, make all fields private and final, and provide only getter methods without any setter methods.

Q5. What is dynamic method dispatch in Java and why is it used?

Answer: Dynamic method dispatch is the process of resolving a method call at runtime rather than compile-time. It occurs when a superclass reference points to a subclass object and an overridden method is invoked. This is used to achieve runtime polymorphism and enables flexibility in code.

Q6. What is the difference between this keyword and the super keyword in Java?

Answer: The this keyword refers to the current instance of the class and is used to access instance variables and methods, or to call another constructor in the same class. The super keyword refers to the parent class and is used to access parent class methods, variables, and constructors.

Q7. What is the purpose of the static keyword in Java?

Answer: The static keyword is used to define class-level variables, methods, blocks, and nested classes. Static members belong to the class rather than any specific instance, meaning they can be accessed without creating an object of the class.

Q8. What is the difference between aggregation and composition in Java?

Answer: Aggregation represents a weak "has-a" relationship where the child object can exist independently of the parent object. Composition represents a strong "has-a" relationship where the child object cannot exist without the parent.

Q9. What are wrapper classes in Java and why are they needed?

Answer: Wrapper classes are used to convert primitive data types into objects. They are needed because Java collections and many APIs work with objects rather than primitive types. Examples include Integer, Double, and Character.

Q10. What is the purpose of the instanceof operator in Java?

Answer: The instanceof operator is used to check whether an object is an instance of a particular class or implements a specific interface. It is useful for avoiding ClassCastException during typecasting.

Chapter 17: Mostly Asked Important Questions – Part M

Q1. What is encapsulation in Java and why is it important?

Answer: Encapsulation is the process of wrapping data (variables) and methods that cperate on the data into a single unit, typically a class. It restricts direct access to certain components by using access modifiers and provides controlled access through getter and setter methods. Encapsulation ensures data security, improves maintainability, and supports abstraction.

Q2. What is abstraction in Java? How is it implemented?

Answer: Abstraction is the concept of hiding implementation details and showing only the essential features of an object. It is implemented in Java using abstract classes and interfaces. Abstract classes can have abstract methods without implementation, and interfaces define a contract that implementing classes must fulfill.

Q3. What is method overriding in Java? Give an example.

Answer: Method overriding occurs when a subclass provides its own implementation of a method that is already defined in the parent class. The overridden method must have the same signature and

Example:

java

CopyEdit

```
class Animal {
  void sound() {
    System.out.println("Animal makes a sound");
  }
}
class Dog extends Animal {
  void sound() {
    System.out.println("Dog barks");
  }
}
```

Q4. What is method overloading in Java? How is it different from overriding?

Answer: Method overloading occurs when multiple methods in the same class have the same name but different parameter lists (different number or type of parameters). It is resolved at compile-time. Overriding happens in inheritance when a subclass redefines a parent class method, and it is resolved at runtime.

Q5. What is inheritance in Java and what are its types?

Answer: Inheritance allows a class to acquire the properties and behaviors of another class. It promotes code reuse and establishes a parent-child relationship. The types of inheritance in Java are single, multilevel, and hierarchical. Java does not support multiple inheritance with classes to avoid ambiguity but supports it with interfaces.

Q6. What is a default constructor in Java and when is it provided?

Answer: A default constructor is a no-argument constructor automatically provided by the Java compiler if no other constructor is defined in the class. It initializes object fields with default values like 0 for numbers and null for objects.

Q7. What is the difference between a local variable, instance variable, and class variable in Java?

Answer: A local variable is declared inside a method and exists only during method execution. An instance variable belongs to an object and each object has its own copy. A class variable (static variable) belongs to the class and is shared among all instances.

Q8. What are static methods in Java? Can they access instance variables?

Answer: Static methods belong to the class and can be called without creating an object. They cannot directly access instance variables because static methods do not operate on specific objects. They can only access other static variables and methods directly.

Q9. What is the use of the final keyword in Java for classes, methods, and variables?

Answer: The final keyword prevents modification. A final variable cannot be reassigned. A final method cannot be overridden in a subclass. A final class cannot be extended. This is useful for enforcing immutability and ensuring certain parts of the code remain unchanged.

Q10. What is the difference between an abstract class and a concrete class in Java?

Answer: An abstract class cannot be instantiated and may have abstract methods without implementation. A concrete class provides complete implementations for all its methods and can be instantiated. Abstract classes are used to provide partial abstraction, while concrete classes represent fully defined objects.

Chapter 18: Mostly Asked Important Questions – Part N

Q1. What is the difference between a class and an object in Java?

Answer: A class is a blueprint or template that defines the structure and behavior of objects. It contains fields (variables) and methods. An object is an instance of a class that has its own state and can use the behaviors defined in the class.

Q2. What are constructors in Java and how are they different from methods?

Answer: Constructors are special methods used to initialize objects when they are created. They have the same name as the class and do not have a return type. Unlike methods, constructors are automatically called when an object is instantiated.

Q3. What is the difference between deep cloning and shallow cloning in Java?

Answer: Shallow cloning copies the fields of an object, but for objects referenced by those fields, it copies only the references and not the actual objects. Deep cloning creates a copy of the object as well as copies of all objects referenced by it, resulting in a fully independent duplicate.

Q4. What is multiple inheritance in Java and how is it achieved?

Answer: Multiple inheritance refers to a class inheriting from more than one parent class. Java does not allow multiple inheritance with classes to avoid ambiguity but achieves it through interfaces. A class can implement multiple interfaces and provide implementations for their methods.

Q5. What is an interface in Java and how is it different from an abstract class?

Answer: An interface is a collection of abstract methods that define a contract for classes to implement. Unlike abstract classes, interfaces cannot have instance variables (except constants) and cannot provide constructors. Abstract classes can have concrete methods and fields, but interfaces allow multiple inheritance.

Q6. What is a package in Java and why is it used?

Answer: A package is a namespace that organizes related classes and interfaces into a single module. It helps avoid name conflicts, improves code organization, and provides controlled access through access modifiers.

Q7. What is the difference between overriding and hiding in Java?

Answer: Overriding happens when a subclass provides its own implementation of a method defined in its parent class. Hiding occurs when a subclass defines a static method with the same signature as a static method in the parent class. Overriding uses dynamic binding, while hiding uses static binding.

Q8. What is the transient keyword in Java?

Answer: The transient keyword is used to indicate that a field should not be serialized. When an object is serialized, transient fields are skipped and not saved in the byte stream. It is useful for sensitive or temporary data.

Q9. What is the volatile keyword in Java?

Answer: The volatile keyword ensures that changes made to a variable by one thread are immediately visible to other threads. It prevents the JVM from caching the variable locally in threads and forces reads and writes to happen directly in main memory.

Q10. What is the difference between String, StringBuilder, and StringBuffer in Java?

Answer: String objects are immutable, meaning their values cannot be changed after creation. StringBuilder and StringBuffer are mutable and allow modification of string data. StringBuilder is not synchronized and is faster, while StringBuffer is synchronized and thread-safe.

Chapter 19: Mostly Asked Important Questions – Part O

Q1. What is the difference between a static class and a non-static class in Java?

Answer: In Java, only nested classes can be declared static. A static nested class does not have access to the instance variables and methods of the outer class unless it has a reference to an instance of the outer class. A non-static nested class (inner class) is associated with an instance of the outer class and can access its instance members directly.

Q2. What is the purpose of a no-argument constructor in Java?

Answer: A no-argument constructor is used to create an object with default values. If no constructor is defined in a class, the compiler automatically provides a default no-argument constructor. If any constructor with arguments is defined, the compiler does not provide a no-argument constructor automatically.

Q3. What is the difference between a Java Bean and a regular Java class?

Answer: A Java Bean follows specific conventions: it must have a no-argument constructor, properties should be private with public getter and setter methods, and it should be serializable. Regular Java classes do not have these strict conventions. Java Beans are mainly used for encapsulating data in reusable components.

Q4. What is the difference between static methods and instance methods in Java?

Answer: Static methods belong to the class and can be called without creating an object. They can only directly access static variables and other static methods. Instance methods belong to objects and can access both instance variables and static variables.

Q5. What is a copy constructor in Java and how is it implemented?

Answer: A copy constructor is a constructor that creates a new object as a copy of an existing object. Java does not provide a default copy constructor, but it can be implemented manually.

Example:

java

CopyEdit

```
class Person {
String name;
Person(Person p) {
this.name = p.name;
}
}
```

Q6. What is an enum in Java and how is it used?

Answer: An enum is a special type in Java used to define a collection of constants. Enums are type-safe and can have fields, constructors, and methods. Example:

java

CopyEdit

```
enum Day {
MONDAY, TUESDAY, WEDNESDAY
}
```

Q7. What is the difference between throw and throws in Java?

Answer: The throw keyword is used to explicitly throw an exception in the code. The throws keyword is used in method declarations to specify which exceptions the method may throw.

Q8. What is the difference between abstract classes and final classes in Java?

Answer: An abstract class cannot be instantiated and may contain abstract methods that must be implemented by subclasses. A final class cannot be extended and prevents inheritance. Abstract classes support partial abstraction, while final classes enforce immutability of the class design.

Q9. What is the difference between a private and a protected member in Java?

Answer: A private member is accessible only within the same class. A protected member is accessible within the same package and in subclasses, even if they are in different packages.

Q10. What is the difference between ArrayList and LinkedList in Java?

Answer: ArrayList is backed by a dynamic array and is better for accessing elements, as it provides constant-time access by index. LinkedList is backed by a doubly linked list and is better for insertions and deletions, especially in the middle of the list, as they require constant time.

Chapter 20: Mostly Asked Important Questions – Part P

Q1. What is the difference between an interface and a marker interface in Java?
Answer: An interface in Java defines a contract with abstract methods that a class must implement. A marker interface, on the other hand, does not contain any methods or fields and serves as a tag or metadata to indicate that a class possesses certain properties. Examples of marker interfaces include Serializable and Cloneable.

Q2. What is the difference between composition and aggregation in Java?
Answer: Both represent relationships between classes. Composition is a strong "has-a" relationship where the contained object cannot exist independently of the container object. Aggregation is a weaker "has-a" relationship where the contained object can exist independently. For example, a "Car has an Engine" (composition), but a "Department has Professors" (aggregation).

Q3. What is method signature in Java and why is it important?
Answer: A method signature consists of the method name and parameter list (number, type, and order of parameters). It uniquely identifies a method within a class and is used by the compiler to resolve method calls. Return type and access modifiers are not part of the method signature.

Q4. What is the difference between static binding and dynamic binding in Java?
Answer: Static binding occurs at compile-time and is used for overloaded methods and static methods. Dynamic binding occurs at runtime and is used for overridden methods, where the method call is resolved based on the actual object type.

Q5. What is object serialization in Java and why is it used?
Answer: Serialization is the process of converting an object into a byte stream so it can be saved to a file, sent over a network, or stored in a database. It is used to persist object states or transfer objects between different Java Virtual Machines (JVMs).

Q6. What is the difference between public static void main(String[] args) and other method signatures in Java?
Answer: This method is the entry point for Java applications. The public modifier allows JVM access, static means it can be called without creating an object, void indicates it returns nothing, and String[] args allows command-line arguments to be passed to the program.

Q7. What is an anonymous class in Java and where is it used?
Answer: An anonymous class is a class without a name that is defined and instantiated in a single expression. It is often used to provide quick implementations of interfaces or abstract classes, especially in GUI applications and event handling.

Q8. What is the difference between equals() and hashCode() methods in Java?

Answer: The equals() method checks if two objects are logically equivalent, while hashCode() returns an integer used in hash-based collections like HashMap. If two objects are equal according to equals(), they must have the same hash code.

Q9. What is the difference between the synchronized keyword and the volatile keyword in Java?

Answer: The synchronized keyword ensures that only one thread can execute a block of code or method at a time, providing mutual exclusion. The volatile keyword ensures that the value of a variable is always read from and written to main memory, guaranteeing visibility but not atomicity.

Q10. What is the difference between a thread and a process in Java?

Answer: A thread is the smallest unit of execution within a process and shares the same memory space as other threads in the process. A process is an independent program with its own memory space. Threads are lightweight compared to processes and are used for concurrent execution within the same application.

Printed at Repro India Ltd.